CW01661800

WILLIAM BARNES

Speech was shapen of the breath-sounds of speakers, for the ears of hearers, and not from speech-tokens (letters) in books . . . and therefore I have shapen my teaching as that of a speech of breath-sounded words, and not of lettered ones.

William Barnes
An Outline of English Speech-Craft

WILLIAM BARNES

Selected Poems

Edited with an introduction and glossary by Robert Nye

FyfieldBooks

Copyright © Robert Nye 1972, 1988
All Rights Reserved

ISBN 0-85635-032-X

First published in 1972
Published in new format 1988 by
Carcanet Press Limited
208–212 Corn Exchange Buildings
Manchester M4 3BQ
and 198 Sixth Avenue
New York, NY 10013

The publisher acknowledges financial assistance
from the Arts Council of Great Britain.

Printed in England by SRP Ltd, Exeter.

To Olwyn Hughes

CONTENTS

EDITOR'S NOTE

The text of the poems in this selection has been drawn from *The Poems of William Barnes,* edited in two volumes by Bernard Jones and published by Centaur Press in 1962. This text corresponds to Barnes's final intentions, for it follows the revisions of the 1879 collected edition, and prints the poet's latest versions in the case of poems in common English reworded after their appearance in the books of 1846 and 1868.

It would be pretentious to speak of a 'bibliography' in a book as small as this, but the interested reader should certainly seek out in a library the main volumes Barnes published in his own lifetime. These are, in verse: *Poems of Rural Life, in the Dorset Dialect* (1844); *Poems, partly of Rural Life* (*In National English*) (1846); *Hwomely Rhymes; A Second Collection of Poems in the Dorset Dialect* (1859); *Poems of Rural Life, in the Dorset Dialect. Third Collection* (1862); *Poems of Rural Life, in Common English* (1868); *A Selection from Unpublished Poems by the Rev. William Barnes* (1870); and the collected edition mentioned above, *Poems of Rural Life, in the Dorset Dialect* (1879). In prose: *A Philological Grammar, grounded upon English, and formed from a comparison of more than Sixty Languages* (1854); *Views of Labour and of Gold* (1859); *Tiw, or a View of the Roots and Stems of the English as a Teutonic Tongue* (1862); *A Grammar and Glossary of the Dorset Dialect* (1864); *Early England and the Saxon English* (1869); *An Outline of English Speech-Craft* (1878); and *An Outline of Rede-Craft* (*Logic*) (1880). There is also some critical writing worth considering: notably two uncollected essays, 'William Barnes' and 'Life of William Barnes', contributed by Coventry Patmore to *St. James's Gazette* in 1886 and 1887, and the same author's 'An English Classic, William Barnes', included in his *Religio Poetae* (1893); Thomas Hardy's preface to his *Select Poems of William Barnes* (1908); Geoffrey Grigson's introduction to his *Selected Poems of William Barnes* (1950); and the essay, 'William Barnes', by C. H. Sisson, in that poet's collection of essays entitled *Art and Action* (1965).

INTRODUCTION

'THE REV. W. Barnes, good soul, of Dorset dialect poems (in which there is more true poetry than there is in Burns).' Thus, Father Hopkins to Doctor Bridges, in a letter dated 26th November, 1882. It is not surprising that Hopkins should have admired Barnes, for they shared a large wish to Saxonise the English language, as well as a smaller one to adopt the tricks of Welsh prosody, especially the *cynghanedd,* into their own verse. The reference to Burns is argumentative and unhelpful, but in another letter to the same correspondent (14th August, 1879) Hopkins has something more interesting to say:

> His poems used to charm me also by their Westcountry 'instress', a most peculiar product of England, which I associate with airs like Weeping Winifred, Polly Oliver, or Poor Mary Ann, with Herrick and Herbert, with the Worcestershire, Herefordshire, and Welsh landscape, and above all with the smell of oxeyes and applelofts: this instress is helped by particular rhythms and these Barnes employs.

The drift of thought there moves discussion of Barnes away from the dialect and into the language, which can be taken as the right direction; he begins to be seen as a man in a particular place who has, as it were, penetrated that place to tap something less limited. The matter of Barnes's Englishness is what should concern those who intend to do him justice. It is impertinent to praise or dismiss him as a 'Dorset' poet, a poet whose relevance and achievement are local; and besides, when that is done the task of assessing his peculiar use of language has hardly been touched. By dubbing that usage 'dialect', in fact, it is possible to ignore the issue of just how good this poet is.

He was born in 1801 at Bagber in the parish of Sturminster Newton in the Vale of Blackmore. His father, John Barnes, was a small farmer. His mother, Grace, died when he was five. Barnes was brought up largely by his aunts. He was educated at the

Church school in Sturminster, leaving it at thirteen to enter a solicitor's office as a clerk. He worked with the village priest in his spare time at classics and also studied music under the organist. When Barnes was seventeen he moved to Dorchester, where he found employment with another solicitor and continued his education with another clergyman. In Dorchester he met Julia Miles, the daughter of an excise officer, and fell in love with her. They became engaged in 1822. In 1823 Barnes went to Mere, in Wiltshire, to run a school. Four years later he married Julia and they set up their home in Chantry House, a Tudor mansion in Mere. They had six children. The schoolmastering went on for nearly forty years, latterly in Dorchester. Julia died in 1852. Four years earlier, at the age of forty-seven, Barnes had taken holy orders. The ten years following Julia's death were difficult ones. His school began to fail, he was beset by acute financial anxieties. Then, in 1862, Barnes was given the living of Winterborne Came, a parish near Dorchester. He lived on for twenty-four years, and was an excellent priest. Thomas Hardy became his neighbour at Max Gate, which stands near the rectory. Barnes died at the age of eighty-five, having composed one of his finest poems, 'The Geäte a-Vallèn To', right at the end, when he was too weak to hold a pen but dictated the lines to his daughter Laura:

There's moon-sheen now in nights o' fall
When leaves be brown vrom green,
When, to the slammen o' the geäte,
Our Jenny's ears be keen,
When the wold dog do wag his taïl,
An' Jeän could tell to who,
As he do come in drough the geäte,
The geäte a-vallèn to.

His daughter reported that he asked her to pay particular attention to the spelling of the word *geäte*. 'That is how King Alfred would have pronounced it,' he said.

Barnes's early poems (the ones he wrote up to about the age

of thirty-three) are in conventional 'national' English, and so are many of the later ones. Some of these – 'Black and White', for example, or 'Troubles of the Day' – are not markedly inferior to his poems in Dorset speech-forms. As to why he used the latter, he has left us two comments. The first of these will be found in the preface to the 1862 collection:

> To write in what some may deem a fast out-wearing speech-form may seem as idle as the writing one's name in the snow of a spring day. I cannot help it. It is my mother tongue, and is to my mind the only true speech of the life that I draw.

We may note the word *mother* and also the impression of a certain literary awkwardness in some of the poems in conventional English. They are bookish, they lack vigour, their refrains seem forced, sometimes divorced from the natural principles which govern turns of speech. Barnes's other comment is in his unpublished 'Notes on the Life of William Barnes', where he declares: 'As to my Dorset poems and others, I wrote them so to say, as if I could not help it, the writing of them was not work but like the playing of music, the refreshment of the mind from care or irksomeness.' Both confessions rest gently on the word *mind.* Barnes, philologist as well as poet, was in search of a shape within English which could contain as much as the Doric within Greek. It appears, indeed, that he took the *Idyllia* of Theocritus quite consciously as an example. He was after a means of marrying metrical structures with natural speech rhythms.

To see how successful he was we have only to look at the eclogues. These are not exercises in quaintness. Barnes is finding a verse which will fit current speech as he has heard it. The attempt should properly be compared with some of Pound's efforts in a similar direction in the *Cantos,* or with Eliot's *Sweeney Agonistes*; most instructively of all, perhaps, with the poems of C. H. Sisson, a poet who is very sensible of what Barnes stands for, and who has himself drawn attention to the opening lines of 'The Common a-Took In':

Good morn t'ye, John. How b'ye? how b'ye?
Zoo you be gwaïn to market, I do zee.
Why, you be quite a-lwoaded wi' your geese.

'It is the very inflection of ordinary speech,' writes Sisson, 'and where else would you look for that in the verse written in England in 1833? It is not in the odd line or two that Barnes has caught it; all the eclogues in his first volume of Dorset poems have it throughout, combined with an utter sureness in the handling of metre. This represents an immense technical liberation, and the poetry of the nineteenth century suffered a progressive softening through lack of attention to it.'*

In passing one could do worse than to recall another remark of Sisson's, made elsewhere: 'The man that was the same in Neolithic and in Roman times, as now, is of more interest than the freak of circumstances. This truth lies at the bottom of a well of rhythm.' William Barnes looked for it through the rhythms he associated with the language of his childhood, and the tangy speech of Blackmore Vale. His problem up to the age of thirty-three must have been to find a language flexible and simple enough to flesh the sense of things expressed in the first fourteen lines of 'The Happy Days When I Wer Young':

In happy days when I wer young,
An' had noo ho, an' laugh'd an' zung,
The maïd wer merry by her cow,
An' men were merry wi' the plough;
But never talk'd, at hwome or out
O' doors, o' what's a-talk'd about
By many now, – that to despise
The laws o' God an' man is wise.
Wi' daily health, an' daily bread,
An' thatch above their shelter'd head,
They velt noo fear, an' had noo spite,
To keep their eyes awake at night;
But slept in peace wi' God on high
An' man below, an' fit to die.

* *Art and Action* (1965), p. 44.

There is such a quiet kind of perfection at work there that we have to look again to notice how telling the twelfth line is.

With great good fortune, or more truly by an act of sustained poetic attention to his roots and his inheritance, Barnes's problem resolved itself: the uncorrupted language he required to re-enter his Eden was the language of that Eden, the speech of Blackmore Vale. His deepest thoughts and feelings came to him at one with the first speech sounds he had heard, as a boy in the parish of Sturminster Newton at the start of the nineteenth century. He described the process in 'The Woody Hollow':

When wrongs an' overbearen words
Do prick my bleeden heart lik' swords,
Then I do try, vor Christes seäke,
To think o' you, sweet days! an' meäke
My soul as 'twer when you did weäke
My childhood's eyes, an' when, if spite
Or grief did come, did die at night
In sleep 'ithin the hollow.

He was never more serious, and when he did see like that, he wrote poems, going back *through* this scrupulous language of Blackmore Vale towards first himself, then something more recalcitrant and persistent and interesting than self. I will not name that something. It is to be found in the poems I have chosen for this little book, most especially in the way they move about the word *ground* – a key word, for Barnes. When he declared his wish 'to purify our tongue and enrich it from its own resources' he said what he knew. In the last reckoning all his learning about language taught him something about the soul's movement in words, its acts of adoration, contrition, thanksgiving, and supplication. It is William Barnes who is purified and clarified in these remarkable poems, not just the dialect of the tribe.

Robert Nye

Edinburgh
June 1972.

THE SPRING

When wintry weather's all a-done,
An' brooks do sparkle in the zun,
An' naïsy-builden rooks do vlee
Wi' sticks toward their elem tree;
When birds do zing, an' we can zee
  Upon the boughs the buds o'spring, –
  Then I'm as happy as a king,
    A-vield wi' health an' zunsheen.

Vor then the cowslip's hangen flow'r
A-wetted in the zunny show'r,
Do grow wi' vi'lets, sweet o' smell,
Bezide the wood-screen'd graegle's bell;
Where drushes' aggs, wi' sky-blue shell,
  Do lie in mossy nest among
  The thorns, while they do zing their zong
    At evenen in the zunsheen.

An' God do meäke his win' to blow
An' raïn to vall vor high an' low,
An' bid his mornen zun to rise
Vor all alike, an' groun' an' skies
Ha' colors vor the poor man's eyes:
  An' in our trials He is near,
  To hear our mwoan an' zee our tear,
    An' turn our clouds to zunsheen.

An' many times when I do vind
Things all goo wrong, an' vo'k unkind,
To zee the happy veeden herds,
An' hear the zingen o' the birds,
Do soothe my sorrow mwore than words;

Vor I do zee that 'tis our sin
Do meäke woone's soul so dark 'ithin,
  When God would gi'e woone zunsheen.

THE WOODLANDS

O spread ageän your leaves an' flow'rs,
  Lwonesome woodlands! zunny woodlands!
Here underneath the dewy show'rs
  O' warm-aïr'd spring-time, zunny woodlands!
As when, in drong or open ground,
Wi' happy bwoyish heart I vound
The twitt'ren birds a-builden round
  Your high-bough'd hedges, zunny woodlands!

You gi'ed me life, you gi'ed me jaÿ,
  Lwonesome woodlands! zunny woodlands!
You gi'ed me health, as in my plaÿ
  I rambled through ye, zunny woodlands!
You gi'ed me freedom, vor to rove
In aïry meäd or sheädy grove;
You gi'ed me smilen Fannèy's love,
  The best ov all o't, zunny woodlands!

My vu'st shrill skylark whiver'd high,
  Lwonesome woodlands! zunny woodlands!
To zing below your deep-blue sky
  An' white spring-clouds, O zunny woodlands!
An' boughs o' trees that woonce stood here,
Wer glossy green the happy year
That gi'ed me woone I lov'd so dear,
  An' now ha' lost, O zunny woodlands!

O let me rove ageän unspied,
    Lwonesome woodlands! zunny woodlands!
Along your green-bough'd hedges' zide,
    As then I rambled, zunny woodlands!
An' where the missen trees woonce stood,
Or tongues woonce run among the wood,
My memory shall meäke em good,
    Though you've a-lost em, zunny woodlands!

EASTER ZUNDAY

Last Easter Jim put on his blue
Frock cwoat, the vu'st time – vier new;
Wi' yollow buttons all o' brass,
That glitter'd in the zun lik' glass;
An' pok'd 'ithin the button-hole
A tutty he'd a-begg'd or stole.
A span-new wes'co't, too, he wore,
Wi' yollow stripes all down avore;
An' tied his breeches' lags below
The knee, wi' ribbon in a bow;
An' drow'd his kitty-boots azide,
An' put his laggens on, an' tied
His shoes wi' strings two vingers wide,
        Because 'twer Easter Zunday.

An' after mornen church wer out
He come back hwome, an' stroll'd about
All down the vields, an' drough the leäne,
Wi' sister Kit an' cousin Jeäne,
A-turnen proudly to their view
His yollow breast an' back o' blue.

The lambs did plaÿ, the grounds wer green,
The trees did bud, the zun did sheen;
The lark did zing below the sky,
An' roads wer all a-blown so dry,
As if the zummer wer begun;
An' he had sich a bit o' fun!
He meäde the maïdens squeäl an' run,
Because 'twer Easter Zunday.

DOCK-LEAVES

The dock-leaves that do spread so wide
Up yonder zunny bank's green zide,
Do bring to mind what we did do
At plaÿ wi' dock-leaves years agoo:
How we, – when nettles had a-stung
Our little hands, when we wer young, –
Did rub 'em wi' a dock, an' zing
'Out nettl', in dock. In dock, out sting.'
An' when your feäce, in zummer's het,
Did sheen wi' tricklen draps o' zweat,
How you, a-zot bezide the bank,
Didst toss your little head, an' pank,
An' teäke a dock-leaf in your han',
An' whisk en lik' a leädy's fan;
While I did hunt, 'ithin your zight,
Vor streaky cockle-shells to fight.

In all our plaÿ-geämes we did bruise
The dock-leaves wi' our nimble shoes;
Bwoth where we merry chaps did fling
You maïdens in the orcha'd swing,
An' by the zaw-pit's dousty bank,

Where we did taït upon a plank.
– (D'ye mind how woonce, you cou'den zit
The bwoard, an' vell off into pit?)
An' when we hunted you about
The grassy barken, in an' out
Among the ricks, your vlee-en frocks
An' nimble veet did strik' the docks.
An' zoo they docks, a-spread so wide
Up yonder zunny bank's green zide,
Do bring to mind what we did do
Among the dock-leaves years agoo.

WOODCOM' FEAST

Come, Fanny, come! put on thy white,
'Tis Woodcom' feäst, good now! to-night.
Come! think noo mwore, you silly maïd,
O' chicken drown'd, or ducks a-straÿ'd;
Nor mwope to vind thy new frock's taïl
A-tore by hitchen in a naïl;
Nor grieve an' hang thy head azide,
A-thinken o' thy lam' that died.
The flag's a-vlee-en wide an' high,
An' ringen bells do sheäke the sky;
The fifes do plaÿ, the horns do roar,
An' boughs be up at ev'ry door:
They'll be a-dancen soon, – the drum
'S a-rumblen now. Come, Fanny, come!
Why father's gone, an' mother too.
They went up leäne an hour agoo;
An' at the green the young an' wold
Do stan' so thick as sheep in vwold:
The men do laugh, the bwoys do shout, –

Come out you mwopen wench, come out,
An' go wi' me, an' show at leäst
Bright eyes an' smiles at Woodcom' feäst.

Come, let's goo out, an' fling our heels
About in jigs an' vow'r-han' reels;
While all the stiff-lagg'd wolder vo'k,
A-zitten roun', do talk an' joke
An' smile to zee their own wold rigs,
A-show'd by our wild geämes an' jigs.
Vor ever since the wold church speer
Vu'st prick'd the clouds, vrom year to year,
When grass in meäd did reach woone's knees,
An' blooth did kern in apple-trees,
Zome merry day 'v' a-broke to sheen
Above the dance at Woodcom' green,
An' all o' they that now do lie
So low all roun' the speer so high,
Woonce, vrom the biggest to the leäst,
Had merry hearts at Woodcom' feäst.

Zoo keep it up, an' gi'e it on
To other vo'k when we be gone.
Come out; vor when the zetten zun
Do leäve in sheäde our harmless fun,
The moon a-risèn in the east
Do gi'e us light at Woodcom' feäst.
Come, Fanny, come! put on thy white,
'Tis merry Woodcom' feäst to-night:
There's nothen vor to mwope about, –
Come-out, you leäzy jeäde, come out!
An' thou wult be, to woone at leäst,
The prettiest maïd at Woodcom' feäst.

VELLEN O' THE TREE

Aye, the girt elem tree out in little hwome-groun'
Wer a-stannen this mornen, an' now's a-cut down.
Aye, the girt elem tree, so big roun' an' so high,
Where the mowers did goo to their drink, an' did lie
In the sheäde ov his head, when the zun at his heighth
Had a-drove em vrom mowen, wi' het an' wi' drith,
Where the haÿ-meäkers put all their picks an' their reäkes,
An' did squot down to snabble their cheese an' their ceäkes,
An' did vill vrom their flaggons their cups wi' their eäle,
An' did meäke theirzelves merry wi' joke and wi' teäle.

Ees, we took up a rwope an' we tied en all round
At the top o'n, wi' woone end a-hangen to ground,
An' we cut, near the ground, his girt stem a'most drough,
An' we bent the wold head o'n wi' woone tug or two;
An' he swaÿ'd all his limbs, an' he nodded his head,
Till he vell away down like a pillar o' lead :
An' as we did run vrom en, there, clwose at our backs,
Oh ! his boughs come to groun' wi' sich whizzes an' cracks;
An' his top wer so lofty that, now he is down,
The stem o'n do reach a'most over the groun'.
Zoo the girt elem tree out in little hwome-groun',
Wer a-stannen this mornen, an' now's a-cut down.

EVENEN IN THE VILLAGE

Now the light o' the west is a-turn'd to gloom,
   An' the men be at hwome vrom ground;
An' the bells be a-zenden all down the Coombe
   From tower, their mwoansome sound.

An' the wind is still,
An' the house-dogs do bark,
An' the rooks be a-vled to the elems high an' dark,
An' the water do roar at mill.

An' the flickeren light drough the window-peäne
Vrom the candle's dull fleäme do shoot,
An' young Jemmy the smith is a-gone down leäne,
A-playèn his shrill-vaïced flute.
An' the miller's man
Do zit down at his ease
On the seat that is under the cluster o' trees,
Wi' his pipe an' his cider can.

THE WOODY HOLLOW

If mem'ry, when our hope's a-gone,
Could bring us dreams to cheat us on,
Ov happiness our hearts voun' true
In years we come too quickly drough;
What days should come to me, but you,
That burn'd my youthvul cheäks wi' zuns
O' zummer, in my playsome runs
About the woody hollow.

When evenen's risèn moon did peep
Down drough the hollow dark an' deep,
Where gigglen sweethearts meäde their vows
In whispers under waggen boughs;
When whisslen bwoys, an' rottlen ploughs
Wer still, an' mothers, wi' their thin
Shrill vaïces, call'd their daughters in,
From walken in the hollow;

What souls should come avore my zight,
But they that had your zummer light?
The litsome younger woones that smil'd
Wi' comely feäzen now a-spweil'd;
Or wolder vo'k, so wise an' mild,
  That I do miss when I do goo
  To zee the pleäce, an' walk down drough
    The lwonesome woody hollow?

When wrongs an' overbearen words
Do prick my bleeden heart lik' swords,
Then I do try, vor Christes seäke,
To think o' you, sweet days! an' meäke
My soul as 'twer when you did weäke
  My childhood's eyes, an' when, if spite
  Or grief did come, did die at night
    In sleep 'ithin the hollow.

ECLOGUE: THE 'LOTMENTS ...

JOHN AND RICHARD

John

Zoo you be in your groun' then, I do zee,
A-worken and a-zingen lik' a bee.
How do it answer? what d'ye think about it?
D'ye think 'tis better wi' it than without it,
A-reck'nen rent, an' time, an' zeed to stock it,
D'ye think that you be any thing in pocket?

Richard

O, 'tis a goodish help to woone, I'm sure o't.
If I had not a-got it, my poor bwones
Would now ha' eäch'd a-craken stwones
Upon the road; I wish I had zome mwore o't.

John

I wish the girt woones had a-got the greäce
To let out land lik' this in ouer pleäce;
But I do fear there'll never be nwone vor us,
An' I can't tell whatever we shall do:
We be a'most a-starven, an' we'd goo
To 'merica, if we'd enough to car us.

Richard

Why 'twer the squire, good now! a worthy man,
That vu'st brought into ouer pleäce the plan;
He zaid he'd let a vew odd eäcres
O' land to us poor leäb'ren men;
An', faïth, he had enough o' teäkers
Vor that, an' twice so much ageän.
Zoo I took zome here, near my hovel,
To exercise my speäde an' shovel;
An' what wi' dungen, diggen up, an' zeeden,
A-thinnen, cleänen, howen up an' weeden,
I, an' the biggest o' the childern too,
Do always vind some useful jobs to do.

John

Aye, wi' a bit o' ground, if woone got any,
Woone's bwoys can soon get out an' eärn a penny;
An' then, by worken, they do learn the vaster
The way to do things when they have a meäster;
Vor woone must know a deäl about the land
Bevore woone's fit to lend a useful hand,
In geärden or a-vield upon a farm.

Richard

An' then the work do keep em out o' harm;
Vor vo'ks that don't do nothen wull be vound

Soon doen woorse than nothen, I'll be bound.
But as vor me, d'ye zee, wi' theäse here bit
O' land, why I have ev'ry thing a'mwost:
Vor I can fatten vowels vor the spit,
Or zell a good fat goose or two to rwoast;
An' have my beäns or cabbage, greens or grass,
Or bit o' wheat, or such my happy feäte is,
That I can keep a little cow, or ass,
An' a vew pigs to eat the little teäties.

John

An' when your pig's a-fatted pretty well
Wi' teäties, or wi' barley an' some bran,
Why you've a-got zome vlitches vor to zell,
Or hang in chimney-corner, if you can.

Richard

Aye, that's the thing; an' when the pig do die,
We got a lot ov offal vor to fry,
An' netlens vor to bwoil; or put the blood in,
An' meäke a meal or two o' good black-pudden.

John

I'd keep myzelf from parish, I'd be bound,
If I could get a little patch o' ground.

ECLOGUE: A BIT O' SLY COORTEN

John and Fanny

John

Now, Fanny, 'tis too bad, you teazen maïd!
How leäte you be a-come! Where have ye staÿ'd?
How long you have a-meäde me waït about!
I thought you werden gwaïn to come ageän.

I had a mind to goo back hwome ageän.
This idden when you promis'd to come out.

Fanny

Now tidden any good to meäke a row,
Upon my word, I cooden come till now.
Vor I've a-been kept in all day by mother,
At work about woone little job an' tother.
If you do want to goo, though, don't ye staÿ
Vor me a minute longer, I do praÿ.

John

I thought you mid be out wi' Jemmy Bleäke.

Fanny

An' why be out wi' him, vor goodness' seäke?

John

You walk'd o' Zunday evenen wi'n, d'ye know,
You went vrom church a-hitched up in his eärm.

Fanny

Well, if I did, that werden any harm.
Lauk! that *is* zome'at to teäke notice o'.

John

He took ye roun' the middle at the stile,
An' kiss'd ye twice 'ithin the ha'f a mile.

Fanny

Ees, at the stile, because I shoulden vall,
He took me hold to help me down, that's all;
An' I can't zee what very mighty harm
He could ha' done a-lenden me his eärm.
An' as vor kissen o' me, if he did,

I didden ax en to, nor zay he mid:
An' if he kiss'd me dree times, or a dozen,
What harm wer it? Why idden he my cousin?
An' I can't zee, then, what there is amiss
In cousin Jem's jist gi'en me a kiss.

John

Well, he shan't kiss ye, then; you shan't be kiss'd
By his girt ugly chops, a lanky houn'!
If I do zee'n, I'll jist wring up my vist
An' knock en down.
I'll squot his girt pug-nose, if I don't miss en;
I'll warn I'll spweil his pretty lips vor kissen!

Fanny

Well, John, I'm sure I little thought to vind
That you had ever sich a jealous mind.
What then! I s'pose that I must be a dummy,
An' mussen goo about nor wag my tongue
To any soul, if he's a man, an' young;
Or else you'll work yourzelf up mad wi' passion,
An' talk away o' gi'en vo'k a drashen,
An' breaken bwones, an' beätèn heads to pummy!
If you've a-got sich jealous ways about ye,
I'm sure I should be better off 'ithout ye.

John

Well, if girt Jemmy have a-won your heart,
We'd better break the coortship off, an' peärt.

Fanny

He won my heart! There, John, don't talk sich stuff;
Don't talk noo mwore, vor you've a-zaid enough.
If I'd a-lik'd another mwore than you,
I'm sure I shoulden come to meet ye zoo;

Vor I've a-twold to father many a storry,
An' took o' mother many a scwolden vor ye.
(*weeping*)
But 'twull be over now, vor you shan't zee me
Out wi' ye noo mwore, to pick a quarrel wi' me.

John

Well, Fanny, I woon't zay noo mwore, my dear.
Let's meäke it up. Come, wipe off thik there tear.
Let's goo an' zit o' top o' theäse here stile,
An' rest, an' look about a little while.

Fanny

Now goo away, you crabbed jealous chap!
You shan't kiss me, – you shan't! I'll gi' ye a slap.

John

Then you look smilen; don't you pout an' toss
Your head so much, an' look so very cross.

Fanny

Now, John! don't squeeze me roun' the middle zoo.
I woon't stop here noo longer, if you do.
Why, John! be quiet, wull ye? Fie upon it!
Now zee how you've a-wrumpl'd up my bonnet!
Mother 'ill zee it after I'm at hwome,
An' gi'e a guess directly how it come.

John

Then don't you zay that I be jealous, Fanny.

Fanny

I wull: vor you *be* jealous, Mister Jahnny.
There's zomebody a-comen down the groun'
Towards the stile. Who is it? Come, get down.

I must run hwome, upon my word then, now;
If I do staÿ, they'll kick up sich a row.
Good night. I can't staÿ now.

John

Then good night, Fanny!
Come out a bit to-morrow evenen, can ye?

ECLOGUE: THE BEST MAN IN THE VIELD

SAM AND BOB

Sam

That's slowish work, Bob. What'st a-been about?
Thy pooken don't goo on not over sprack.
Why I've a-pook'd my weäle, lo'k zee, clear out,
An' here I be ageän a-turnen back.

Bob

I'll work wi' thee then, Sammy, any day,
At any work dost like to teäke me at,
Vor any money thou dost like to lay.
Now, Mister Sammy, what dost think o' that?
My weäle is nearly twice so big as thine,
Or else, I warnt, I shoudden be behin'.

Sam

Ah! hang thee, Bob! don't tell sich whoppen lies.
My weäle's the biggest, if do come to size.
'Tis jist the seäme whatever bist about;
Why, when dost goo a-tedden grass, you sloth,
Another hand's a-fwo'c'd to teäke thy zwath,
An' ted a half way back to help thee out;

An' then a-reäken rollers, bist so slack,
Dost keep the very bwoys an' women back.
An' if thou dost think that thou canst challenge I
At any thing, – then, Bob, we'll teäke a pick a-piece,
An' woonce theäse zummer, goo an' try
To meäke a rick a-piece.
A rick o' thine wull look a little funny,
When thou'st a-done en, I'll bet any money.

Bob

You noggerhead! last year thou meäd'st a rick,
An' then we had to trig en wi' a stick.
An' what did John that tipp'd en zay? Why zaid
He stood a-top o'en all the while in dread,
A-thinken that avore he should a-done en,
He'd tumble over slap wi' him upon en.

Sam

You yoppen dog! I warnt I meäde my rick
So well's thou meädst thy lwoad o' haÿ last week.
They hadden got a hundred yards to haul en,
An' then they vound 'twer best to have en boun',
Vor if they hadden, 'twould a-tumbl'd down;
An' after that I zeed en all but vallèn,
An' trigg'd en up wi' woone o'm's pitchen pick,
To zee if I could meäke en ride to rick;
An' when they had the dumpy heap unboun',
He vell to pieces flat upon the groun'.

Bob

Do shut thy lyen chops! Whot dosten mind
Thy pitchen to me out in Gully-plot,
A meäken o' me waït (wast zoo behind)
A half an hour vor ev'ry pitch I got?
An' how didst groun' thy pick? an' how didst quirk

To get en up on end? Why hadst hard work
To rise a pitch that wer about so big
'S a goodish crow's nest, or a wold man's wig!
Why bist so weak, dost know, as any roller:
Zome o' the women vo'k will beät thee hollor.

Sam

You snub-nos'd flopperchops! I pitch'd so quick,
That thou dost know thou hadst a hardish job
To teäke in all the pitches off my pick;
An' dissen zee me groun' en, nother, Bob.
An' thou bist stronger, thou dost think, than I?
Girt bandy-lags! I jist should like to try.
We'll goo, if thou dost like, an' jist zee which
Can heave the mwost, or car the biggest nitch.

Bob

There, Sam, do meäke me zick to hear thy braggen!
Why bissen strong enough to car a flagon.

Sam

You grinnen fool! why I'd zet thee a-blowen,
If thou wast wi' me vor a day a-mowen.
I'd wear my cwoat, an' thou midst pull thy rags off,
An' then in half a zwath I'd mow thy lags off.

Bob

Thee mow wi' me! Why coossen keep up wi' me:
Why bissen fit to goo a-vield to skimmy,
Or mow down docks an' thistles! Why I'll bet
A shillen, Samuel, that thou cassen whet.

Sam

Now don't thee zay much mwore than what'st a-zaid,
Or else I'll knock thee down, heels over head.

Bob

Thou knock me down, indeed! Why cassen gi'e
A blow half hard enough to kill a bee.

Sam

Well, thou shalt veel upon thy chops and snout.

Bob

Come on then, Samel; jist let's have woone bout.

THE CLOTE
WATER-LILY

O zummer clote! when the brook's a-gliden
   So slow an' smooth down his zedgy bed,
Upon thy broad leaves so seäfe a-riden
   The water's top wi' thy yellow head,
         By alder's heads, O,
         An' bulrush beds, O,
Thou then dost float, goolden zummer clote!

The grey-bough'd withy's a-leänen lowly
   Above the water thy leaves do hide;
The benden bulrush, a-swaÿen slowly,
   Do skirt in zummer thy river's zide;
         An' perch in shoals, O,
         Do vill the holes, O,
Where thou dost float, goolden zummer clote!

Oh! when thy brook-drinken flow'r's a-blowen,
   The burnen zummer's a-zetten in;
The time o' greenness, the time o' mowen,
   When in the hay-vield, wi' zunburnt skin,

The vo'k do drink, O,
Upon the brink, O,
Where thou dost float, goolden zummer clote!

Wi' eärms a-spreaden, an' cheäks a-blowen,
How proud wer I when I vu'st could zwim
Athirt the pleäce where thou bist a-growen,
Wi' thy long more vrom the bottom dim;
While cows, knee-high, O,
In brook, wer nigh, O,
Where thou dost float, goolden zummer clote!

Ov all the brooks drough the meäds a-winden,
Ov all the meäds by a river's brim,
There's nwone so feäir o' my own heart's vinden,
As where the maïdens do zee thee zwim,
An' stan' to teäke, O,
Wi' long-stemm'd reäke, O,
Thy flow'r afloat, goolden zummer clote!

BE'MI'STER

Sweet Be'mi'ster, that bist a-bound
By green an' woody hills all round,
Wi' hedges reachen up between
A thousan' vields o' zummer green,
Where elems' lofty heads do drow
Their sheädes vor haÿ-meäkers below,
An' wild hedge-flow'rs do charm the souls
O' maïdens in their evenen strolls.

When I o' Zunday nights wi' Jeäne
Do saunter drough a vield or leäne,

Where elder-blossoms be a-spread
Above the eltrot's milk-white head,
An' flow'rs o' blackberries do blow
Upon the brembles, white as snow,
To be outdone avore my zight
By Jeäne's gaÿ frock o' dazzlen white;

Oh! then there's nothen that's 'ithout
Thy hills that I do ho about, –
Noo bigger pleäce, noo gaÿer town,
Beyond thy sweet bells' dyen soun',
As they do ring, or strike the hour,
At evenen vrom thy wold red tow'r.
No: shelter still my head, an' keep
My bwones when I do vall asleep.

ECLOGUE: THE VEAIRIES

SIMON AN' SAMEL

Simon

There's what the vo'k do call a veäiry ring
Out there, lo'k zee. Why, 'tis an oddish thing.

Samel

Ah! zoo do seem. I wonder how do come!
What is it that do meäke it, I do wonder?

Simon

Be hang'd if I can tell, I'm sure! But zome
Do zay do come by lightnen when do thunder;
An' zome do say sich rings as thik ring there is,
Do grow in dancen-tracks o' little veäiries,
That in the nights o' zummer or o' spring
Do come by moonlight, when noo other veet

Do tread the dewy grass, but theirs, an' meet
An' dance away together in a ring.

Samel

An' who d'ye think do work the fiddlestick?
A little veäiry too, or else wold Nick!

Simon

Why, they do zay, that at the veäiries' ball,
There's nar a fiddle that's a-heär'd at all;
But they do plaÿ upon a little pipe
A-meäde o' kexes or o' straws, dead ripe,
A-stuck in row (zome short an' longer zome)
Wi' slime o' snaïls, or bits o' plum-tree gum,
An' meäke sich music that to hear it sound,
You'd stick so still's a pollard to the ground.

Samel

What do em dance? 'Tis plaïn by theäse green wheels,
They don't frisk in an' out in dree-hand reels;
Vor else, instead o' theäse here girt round O,
They'd cut us out a figure aïght, d'ye know.

Simon

Oh! they ha' jigs to fit their little veet.
They woulden dance, you know, at their fine ball,
The dree an' vow'r han' reels that we do sprawl
An' kick about in, when we men do meet.

Samel

An' zoo have zome vo'k, in their midnight rambles,
A-catch'd the veäiries, then, in theäsem gambols?

Simon

Why, yes; but they be off lik' any shot,
So soon's a man's a-comen near the spot.

Samel

But in the day-time where do veäiries hide?
Where be their hwomes, then? where do veäiries bide?

Simon

Oh! they do get awaÿ down under ground,
In hollow pleäzen where they can't be vound.
But still my gramfer, many years agoo,
(He liv'd at Grenley-farm, an' milk'd a deäiry),
If what the wolder vo'k do tell is true,
Woone mornen early vound a veäiry.

Samel

An' did he stop, then, wi' the good wold bwoy?
Or did he soon contrive to slip awoy?

Simon

Why, when the vo'k were all asleep, a-bed,
The veäiries us'd to come, as 'tis a-zaid,
Avore the vire wer cwold, an' dance an hour
Or two at dead o' night upon the vloor;
Var they, by only utteren a word
Or charm, can come down chimney lik' a bird;
Or draw their bodies out so long an' narrow,
That they can vlee drough keyholes lik' an arrow.
An' zoo woone midnight, when the moon did drow
His light drough window, roun' the vloor below,
An' crickets roun' the bricken he'th did zing,
They come an' danced about the hall in ring;
An' tapp'd, drough little holes noo eyes could spy,
A kag o' poor aunt's meäd a-stannen by.
An' woone o'm drink'd so much, he coulden mind
The word he wer to zay to meäke en small;

He got a-dather'd zoo, that after all
Out tothers went an' left en back behind.
An' after he'd a-beät about his head,
Ageän the keyhole till he wer half dead,
He laid down all along upon the vloor
Till gramfer, comen down, unlocked the door :
An' then he zeed en ('twer enough to frighten en)
Bolt out o' the door, an' down the road lik' lightenen.

CORN A-TURNEN YOLLOW

The windless copse ha' sheädy boughs,
  Wi' blackbirds' evenen whistles;
The hills ha' sheep upon their brows,
  The zummerleäze ha' thistles :
The meäds be gaÿ in grassy Maÿ,
  But, oh ! vrom hill to hollow,
Let me look down upon a groun'
  O' corn a-turnen yollow.

An' pease do grow in tangled beds,
  An' beäns be sweet to snuff, O;
The teäper woats do bend their heads,
  The barley's beard is rough, O.
The turnip green is fresh between
  The corn in hill or hollow,
But I'd look down upon a groun'
  O' wheat a-turnen yollow.

'Tis merry when the brawny men
  Do come to reap it down, O,
Where glossy red the poppy head
  'S among the stalks so brown, O.

'Tis merry while the wheat's in hile,
  Or when, by hill or hollow,
The leäzers thick do stoop to pick
  The ears so ripe an' yollow.

ECLOGUE: THE COMMON A-TOOK IN

THOMAS AN' JOHN

Thomas

Good morn t'ye, John. How b'ye? how b'ye?
Zoo you be gwaïn to market, I do zee.
Why, you be quite a-lwoaded wi' your geese.

John

Ees, Thomas, ees.
Why, I'm a-getten rid ov ev'ry goose
An' goslen I've a-got: an' what is woose,
I fear that I must zell my little cow.

Thomas

How zoo, then, John? Why, what's the matter now?
What, can't ye get along? B'ye run a-ground?
An' can't paÿ twenty shillens vor a pound?
What, can't ye put a lwoaf on shelf?

John

                                        Ees, now;
But I do fear I shan't 'ithout my cow.
No; they do meän to teäke the moor in, I do hear,
An' 'twill be soon begun upon;
Zoo I must zell my bit o' stock to-year,
Because they woon't have any groun' to run upon.

Thomas

Why, what d'ye tell o'? I be very zorry
To hear what they be gwaïn about;
But yet I s'pose there'll be a 'lotment vor ye,
When they do come to mark it out.

John

No; not vor me, I fear. An' if there should,
Why 'twoulden be so handy as 'tis now;
Vor 'tis the common that do do me good,
The run vor my vew geese, or vor my cow.

Thomas

Ees, that's the job; why 'tis a handy thing
To have a bit o' common, I do know,
To put a little cow upon in Spring,
The while woone's bit ov orcha'd grass do grow.

John

Aye, that's the thing, you zee. Now I do mow
My bit o' grass, an' meäke a little rick;
An' in the zummer, while do grow,
My cow do run in common vor to pick
A bleäde or two o' grass, if she can vind em,
Vor tother cattle don't leäve much behind em.
Zoo in the evenen, we do put a lock
O' nice fresh grass avore the wicket;
An' she do come at vive or zix o'clock,
As constant as the zun, to pick it.
An' then, bezides the cow, why we do let
Our geese run out among the emmet hills;
An' then when we do pluck em, we do get
Vor zeäle zome veathers an' zome quills;
An' in the winter we do fat em well,

An' car em to the market vor to zell
To gentlevo'ks, vor we don't oft avvword
To put a goose a-top ov ouer bwoard;
But we do get our feäst, – vor we be eäble
To clap the giblets up a-top o' teäble.

Thomas

An' I don't know o' many better things,
Than geese's heads and gizzards, lags an' wings.

John

An' then, when I ha' nothen else to do,
Why I can teäke my hook an' gloves, an' goo
To cut a lot o' vuzz and briars
Vor heten ovens, or vor lighten viers.
An' when the childern be too young to eärn
A penny, they can g'out in zunny weather,
An' run about, an' get together
A bag o' cow-dung vor to burn.

Thomas

'Tis handy to live near a common;
But I've a-zeed, an' I've a-zaid,
That if a poor man got a bit o'bread,
They'll try to teäke it vrom en.
But I wer twold back tother day,
That they be got into a way
O' letten bits o' groun out to the poor.

John

Well, I do hope 'tis true, I'm sure;
An' I do hope that they will do it here,
Or I must goo to workhouse, I do fear.

THE HAPPY DAYS WHEN I WER YOUNG

In happy days when I wer young,
An' had noo ho, an' laugh'd an' zung,
The maïd wer merry by her cow,
An' men wer merry wi' the plough;
But never talk'd, at hwome or out
O' doors, o' what's a-talked about
By many now, – that to despise
The laws o' God an' man is wise.
Wi' daily health, an' daily bread,
An' thatch above their shelter'd head,
They velt noo fear, an' had noo spite,
To keep their eyes awake at night;
But slept in peace wi' God on high
An' man below, an' fit to die.

O grassy meäd an' woody nook,
An' waters o' the winden brook,
That sprung below the vu'st dark sky
That raïn'd, to run till seas be dry;
An' hills a-stannen on while all
The works o' man do rise an' vall;
An' trees the toddlen child do vind
At vu'st, an' leäve at last behind;
I wish that you could now unvwold
The peace an' jaÿ o' times o' wold;
An' tell, when death do still my tongue,
O' happy days when I wer young.
Vrom where wer all this venom brought,
To kill our hope an' taïnt our thought?
Clear brook! thy water coulden bring
Such venom vrom thy rocky spring;
Nor could it come in zummer blights,

Or reäven storms o' winter nights,
Or in the cloud an' viry stroke
O' thunder that do split the woak.

O valley dear! I wish that I
'D a-liv'd in former times, to die
Wi' all the happy souls that trod
Thy turf in peäce, an' died to God;
Or gone wi' them that laugh'd an' zung
In happy days when I wer young!

LULLABY

The rook's nest do rock on the tree-top
Where vew foes can stand;
The martin's is high, an' is deep
In the steep cliff o' zand.
But thou, love, a-sleepen where vootsteps
Mid come to thy bed,
Hast father an' mother to watch thee
An' shelter thy head.
    Lullaby, Lilybrow. Lie asleep;
    Blest be thy rest.

An' zome birds do keep under ruffen
Their young vrom the storm,
An' zome wi' nest-hoodens o' moss
An' o' wool, do lie warm.
An' we wull look well to the houseruf
That o'er thee mid leäk,
An' the blast that mid beät on thy windor
Shall not smite thy cheäk.
    Lullaby, Lilybrow. Lie asleep;
    Blest be thy rest.

ECLOGUE: A GHOST
JEM AN' DICK

Jem

This is a darkish evenen; b'ye afeärd
O' zights? Theäse leän's a-haunted, I've a-heärd.

Dick

No, I ben't much afeärd. If vo'k don't strive
To over-reach me while they be alive,
I don't much think the dead wull ha' the will
To come back here to do me any ill.
An' I've a-been about all night, d'ye know,
Vrom candle-lighten till the cock did crow;
But never met wi' nothen bad enough
To be much wo'se than what I be myzuf;
Though I, lik' others, have a-heärd vo'k zay
The girt house is a-haunted, night an' day.

Jem

Aye; I do mind woone winter 'twer a-zaid
The farmer's vo'k could hardly sleep a-bed,
They heärd at night such scuffens an' such jumpens,
Such ugly naïses an' such rottlen thumpens.

Dick

Aye, I do mind I heärd his son, young Sammy,
Tell how the chairs did dance an' doors did slammy;
He stood to it – though zome vo'k woulden heed en –
He didden only hear the ghost, but zeed en;
An', hang me! if I han't a'most a-shook,
To hear en tell what ugly sheäpes it took.
Did zometimes come vull six veet high, or higher,
In white, he zaid, wi' eyes lik' coals o' vier;

An' zometimes, wi' a feäce so peäle as milk,
A smileless leädy, all a-deck'd in silk.
His heäir, he zaid, did use to stand upright,
So stiff's a bunch o' rushes, wi' his fright.

Jem
An' then you know that zome'hat is a-zeed
Down there in leäne, an' over in the meäd,
A-comen zometimes lik' a slinken hound,
Or rollen lik' a vleece along the ground.
An' woonce, when gramfer wi' his wold grey meäre
Wer riden down the leäne vrom Shroton feäir,
It roll'd so big's a pack ov wool across
The road just under en, an' leäm'd his hoss.

Dick
Aye; did ye hear that – vo'k zaid 'twer true –
O' what bevell Jack Hine zome years agoo?
Woone vrosty night, d'ye know, at Chris'mas tide,
Jack, an' another chap or two bezide,
'D a-been out, zomewhere up at tother end
O' parish, to a naïghbour's house to spend
A merry hour, an' mid a-took a cup
Or two o' eäle a-keepen Chris'mas up;
Zoo I do lot 'twer leäte avore the peärty
'D a-burnt their bron out; I do lot, avore
They thought o' turnen out o' door
'Twer mornen, vor their friendship then wer hearty.
Well; clwose ageän the vootpath that do leäd
Vrom higher parish over withy-meäd,
There's still a hollow, you do know : they tried there,
In former times, to meäke a cattle-pit,
But gi'ed it up, because they coulden get
The water any time to bide there.
Zoo when the merry fellows got

Just overright theäse lwonesome spot,
Jack zeed a girt big house-dog wi' a collar,
A-stannen down in thik there hollor.
Lo'k there, he zaid, there's zome girt dog a-prowlen :
I'll just goo down an' gi'en a goodish lick
Or two wi' theäse here groun'-ash stick,
An' zend the shaggy rascal hwome a-howlen.
Zoo there he run, an' gi'ed en a good whack
Wi' his girt ashen stick athirt his back;
An', all at woonce, his stick split right all down
In vower pieces; an' the pieces vled
Out ov his hand all up above his head,
An' pitch'd in vower corners o' the groun'.
An' then he velt his han' get all so num',
He coulden veel a vinger or a thum';
An' after that his eärm begun to zwell,
An' in the night a-bed he vound
The skin o't peelen off all round.
'Twer near a month avore he got it well.

Jem

That wer vor hetten o'n. He should a-let en
Alwone d'ye zee : 'twer wicked vor to het en.

THE HWOMESTEAD

If I had all the land my zight
   Can overlook vrom Chalwell hill,
Vrom Sherborn left to Blanvord right,
   Why I could be but happy still.
An' I be happy wi' my spot
O' freehold ground an' mossy cot,
An' shoulden get a better lot
   If I had all my will.

My orcha'd's wide, my trees be young;
  An' they do bear such heavy crops,
Their boughs, lik' onion rwopes a-hung,
  Be all a-trigg'd to-year, wi' props.
I got some geärden groun' to dig,
A parrock, an' a cow an' pig;
I got zome cider vor to swig,
  An' eäle o' malt an' hops.

I'm landlord o' my little farm,
  I'm king 'ithin my little pleäce;
I don't break laws, an' don't do harm,
  An' ben't afeärd o' noo man's feäce.
When I'm a-cover'd wi' my thatch,
Noo man do deäre to lift my latch;
Where honest han's do shut the hatch,
  There fear do leäve the pleäce.

My lofty elem trees do screen
  My brown-ruf'd house, an' here below,
My geese do strut athirt the green,
  An' hiss an' flap their wings o' snow;
As I do walk along a rank
Ov apple trees, or by a bank,
Or zit upon a bar or plank,
  To zee how things do grow.

A WITCH

There's thik wold hag, Moll Brown, look zee, jus' past!
I wish the ugly sly wold witch
Would tumble over into ditch;
I woulden pull her out not very vast.

No, no. I don't think she's a bit belied,
No, she's a witch; aye, Molly's evil-eyed.
Vor I do know o' many a withren blight
A-cast on vo'k by Molly's mutter'd spite;
She did, woone time, a dreadvul deäl o' harm
To Farmer Gruff's vo'k, down at Lower Farm.
Vor there, woone day, they happened to offend her,
An' not a little to their sorrow,
Because they woulden gi'e or lend her
Zome'hat she come to bag or borrow;
An' zoo, they soon began to vind
That she'd a-gone an' left behind
Her evil wish, that had such pow'r
That she did meäke their milk an' eäle turn zour,
An' addle all the aggs their vowls did lay;
They coulden vetch the butter in the churn,
An' all the cheese begun to turn
All back ageän to curds an' whey;
The little pigs, a-runnen wi' the zow,
Did zicken, zomehow, noobody know'd how,
An' vall, an' turn their snouts toward the sky,
An' only gi'e woone little grunt, an' die;
An' all the little ducks an' chicken
Wer death-struck out in yard a-picken
Their bits o' food, an' vell upon their head,
An' flapp'd their little wings an' drapp'd down dead.
They coulden fat the calves, they woulden thrive;
They coulden seäve their lambs alive;
Their sheep were all a-coath'd, or gi'ed noo wool;
The hosses vell away to skin an' bwones,
An' got so weak they coulden pull
A half a peck o' stwones:
The dog got dead-alive an' drowsy,
The cat vell zick an' woulden mousy;

An' every time the vo'k went up to bed,
They wer a-hag-rod till they wer half dead.
They us'd to keep her out o' house, 'tis true,
A-naïlen up at door a hosses shoe;
An' I've a-heärd the farmer's wife did try
To dawk a needle or a pin
In drough her wold hard wither'd skin,
An' draw her blood, a-comen by:
But she could never vetch a drap,
For pins would ply an' needles snap
Ageän her skin; an' that, in coo'se,
Did meäke the hag bewitch em woo'se.

THE WOLD WAGGON

The girt wold waggon uncle had,
When I wer up a hardish lad,
Did stand, a-screen'd vrom het an' wet,
In zummer at the barken geäte,
Below the elems' spreaden boughs,
A-rubb'd by all the pigs an' cows.
An' I've a-clom his head an' zides,
A-riggen up or jumpen down
A-plaÿen, or in happy rides
Along the leäne or drough the groun'.
An' many souls be in their greäves,
That rod' together on his reäves;
An' he, an' all the hosses too,
'V a-ben a-done vor years agoo.

Upon his head an' taïl wer pinks,
A-païnted all in tangled links;
His two long zides wer blue, – his bed
Bent slightly upward at the head;

His reäves rose upward in a bow
Above the slow hind-wheels below.
Vour hosses wer a-kept to pull
The girt wold waggon when 'twer vull:
The black meäre *Smiler*, strong enough
To pull a house down by herzuf,
So big, as took my widest strides
To straddle halfway down her zides;
An' champen *Vi'let*, sprack an' light,
That foam'd an' pull'd wi' all her might:
An' *Whitevoot*, leäzy in the treäce,
Wi' cunnen looks an' snow-white feäce;
Bezides a baÿ woone, short-taïl *Jack*,
That wer a treäce-hoss or a hack.

How many lwoads o' vuzz, to scald
The milk, thik waggon have a-haul'd!
An' wood vrom copse, an' poles vor raïls,
An' bavens wi' their bushy taïls;
An' loose-ear'd barley, hangen down
Outside the wheels a'most to groun',
An' lwoads o' haÿ so sweet an' dry,
A-builded straïght, an' long, an' high;
An' haÿ-meäkers, a-zitten roun'
The reäves, a-riden hwome vrom groun',
When Jim gi'ed Jenny's lips a smack,
An' jealous Dicky whipp'd his back,
An' maïdens scream'd to veel the thumps
A-gi'ed by trenches an' by humps.
But he, an' all his hosses too,
'V a-ben a-done vor years agoo.

MY ORCHA'D IN LINDEN LEA

'Ithin the woodlands, flow'ry gleäded,
By the woak tree's mossy moot,
The sheenen grass-bleädes, timber-sheäded,
Now do quiver under voot;
An' birds do whissle over head,
An' water's bubblen in its bed,
An' there vor me the apple tree
Do leän down low in Linden Lea.

When leaves that leätely wer a-springen
Now do feäde 'ithin the copse,
An' païnted birds do hush their zingen
Up upon the timber's tops;
An' brown-leav'd fruit's a-turnen red,
In cloudless zunsheen, over head,
Wi' fruit vor me, the apple tree
Do leän down low in Linden Lea.

Let other vo'k meäke money vaster
In the aïr o' dark-room'd towns,
I don't dread a peevish meäster;
Though noo man do heed my frowns,
I be free to goo abrode,
Or teäke ageän my homeward road
To where, vor me, the apple tree
Do leän down low in Linden Lea.

THE WOLD WALL

Here, Jeäne, we vu'st did meet below
The leafy boughs, a-swingen slow,
Avore the zun, wi 'evenen glow,
Above our road, a-beamen red;
The grass in zwath wer in the meäds,
The water gleam'd among the reeds
In aïr a-steälen roun' the hall,
Where ivy clung upon the wall.
Ah! well-a-day! O wall adieu!
The wall is wold, my grief is new.

An' there you walk'd wi' blushen pride,
Where softly-wheelen streams did glide,
Drough sheädes o' poplars at my zide,
An' there wi' love that still do live,
Your feäce did wear the smile o' youth,
The while you spoke wi' age's truth,
An' wi' a rwosebud's mossy ball
I deck'd your bosom vrom the wall.
Ah! well-a-day! O wall adieu!
The wall is wold, my grief is new.

But now when winter's raïn do vall,
An' wind do beät ageän the hall,
The while upon the wat'ry wall
In spots o' grey the moss do grow,
The ruf noo mwore shall overspread
The pillor ov our weary head,
Nor shall the rwose's mossy ball
Behang vor you the house's wall.
Ah! well-a-day! O wall adieu!
The wall is wold, my grief is new.

THE LEANE

They do zay that a travellen chap
   Have a-put in the newspeäper now,
That the bit o' green ground on the knap
   Should be all a-took in vor the plough.
He do fancy 'tis easy to show
   That we can be but stunpolls at best,
Vor to leäve a green spot where a flower can grow,
   Or a voot-weary walker mid rest.
'Tis hedge-grubben, Thomas, an' ledge-grubben,
            Never a-done
While a sov'ren mwore's to be won.

The road, he do zay, is so wide
   As 'tis wanted vor travellers' wheels,
As if all that did travel did ride
   An' did never get galls on their heels.
He would leäve sich a thin strip o' groun',
   That, if a man's veet in his shoes
Wer a-burnen an' zore, why he coulden zit down
   But the wheels would run over his tooes.
Vor 'tis meäke money, Thomas, an' teäke money,
            What's zwold an' bought
Is all that is worthy o' thought.

Years agoo the leäne-zides did bear grass,
   Vor to pull wi' the geeses' red bills,
That did hiss at the vo'k that did pass,
   Or the bwoys that pick'd up their white quills.
But shortly, if vower or vive
   Ov our goslens do creep vrom the agg,
They must mwope in the geärden, mwore dead than alive,
   In a coop, or a-tied by the lag.

Vor to catch at land, Thomas, an' snatch at land,
Now is the plan;
Meäke money wherever you can.

The childern wull soon have noo pleäce
Vor to play in, an' if they do grow,
They wull have a thin musheroom feäce,
Wi' their bodies so sumple as dough.
But a man is a-meäde ov a child,
An' his limbs do grow worksome by plaÿ;
An' if the young child's little body's a-spweil'd,
Why, the man's wull the sooner decaÿ.
But wealth is wo'th now mwore than health is wo'th;
Let it all goo,
If't 'ull bring but a sov'ren or two.

Vor to breed the young fox or the heäre,
We can gi'e up whole eäcres o' ground,
But the greens be a-grudg'd, vor to rear
Our young childern up healthy an' sound;
Why, there woon't be a-left the next age
A green spot where their veet can goo free;
An' the goocoo wull soon be committed to cage
Vor a trespass in zomebody's tree.
Vor 'tis locken up, Thomas, an' blocken up,
Stranger or brother,
Men mussen come nigh woone another.

Woone day I went in at a geäte,
Wi' my child, where an echo did sound,
An' the owner came up, an' did reäte
Me as if I would car off his ground.
But his vield an' the grass wer a-let,
An' the damage that he could a-took

Wer at mwost that the while I did open the geäte
   I did rub roun' the eye on the hook.
But 'tis drevèn out, Thomas, an' heven out.
                  Trample noo grounds,
Unless you be after the hounds.

Ah! the Squier a' Culver-dell Hall
   Wer as diff'rent as light is vrom dark,
Wi' zome vo'k that, as evenen did vall,
   Had a-broke drough long grass in his park;
Vor he went, wi' a smile, vor to meet
   Wi' the trespassers while they did pass,
An' he zaid, 'I do fear you'll catch cwold in your veet,
   You've a-walk'd drough so much o' my grass.'
His mild words, Thomas, cut em like swords, Thomas,
                  Newly a-whet,
An' went vurder wi' them than a dreat.

THE WATER CROWVOOT

O small-feäc'd flow'r that now dost bloom
To stud wi' white the shallow Frome,
An' leäve the clote to spread his flow'r
On darksome pools o' stwoneless Stour,
When sof'ly rizèn aïrs do cool
The water in the sheenen pool,
Thy beds o' snow-white buds do gleam
So feäir upon the sky-blue stream,
As whitest clouds, a-hangen high
Avore the blueness o' the sky;
An' there, at hand, the thin heäir'd cows,
In aïry sheädes o' withy boughs,
Or up bezide the mossy raïls,
Do stan', an' zwing their heavy tails,

The while the ripplen stream do flow
Below the dousty bridge's bow;
An' quiv'ren water-gleams do mock
The weäves, upon the sheäded rock;
An' up athirt the copen stwone
The laïtren bwoy do leän alwone,
A-watchen, wi' a stedvast look,
The vallèn waters in the brook,
The while the zand o' time do run
An' leäve his errand still undone.
An' oh! as long's thy buds would gleam
Above the softly-sliden stream,
While sparklen zummer-brooks do run
Below the lofty-climen zun,
I only wish that thou could'st staÿ
Vor noo man's harm, an' all men's jaÿ.
But no, the waterman 'ull weäde
Thy water wi' his deadly bleäde,
To slaÿ thee even in thy bloom,
Fair small-feäc'd flow'r o' the Frome.

FALSE FRIENDS-LIKE

When I wer still a bwoy, an' mother's pride,
A bigger bwoy spoke up to me so kind-like,
'If you do like, I'll treat ye wi' a ride
In theäse wheel-barrow here.' Zoo I wer blind-like
To what he had a-worken in his mind-like,
An' mounted vor a passenger inside;
An' comen to a puddle, perty wide,
He tipp'd me in, a-grinnen back behind-like.
Zoo when a man do come to me so thick-like,
An' sheäke my hand, where woonce he pass'd me by,

An' tell me he would do me this or that,
I can't help thinken o' the big bwoy's trick-like.
An' then, vor all I can but wag my hat
An' thank en, I do veel a little shy.

THE WIFE A-LOST

Since I noo mwore do zee your feäce,
    Up steäirs or down below,
I'll zit me in the lwonesome pleäce,
    Where flat-bough'd beech do grow;
Below the beeches' bough, my love,
    Where you did never come,
An' I don't look to meet ye now,
    As I do look at hwome.

Since you noo mwore be at my zide,
    In walks in zummer het,
I'll goo alwone where mist do ride,
    Drough trees a-drippen wet;
Below the raïn-wet bough, my love,
    Where you did never come,
An' I don't grieve to miss ye now,
    As I do grieve at hwome.

Since now bezide my dinner-bwoard
    Your vaïce do never sound,
I'll eat the bit I can avvword,
    A-yield upon the ground;
Below the darksome bough, my love,
    Where you did never dine,
An' I don't grieve to miss ye now,
    As I at hwome do pine.

Since I do miss your vaïce an' feäce
        In praÿer at eventide,
I'll praÿ wi' woone sad vaïce vor greäce
        To goo where you do bide;
Above the tree an' bough, my love,
        Where you be gone avore,
An' be a waïten vor me now,
        To come vor evermore.

THE HEARE

Dree o'm a-ta'kèn o't.

(1) There be the greyhounds! lo'k! an' there's the heäre!
(2) What houn's, the squier's, Thomas? where, then, where?
(1) Why, out in Ash Hill, near the barn, behind
    Thik tree.
                    (3) The pollard?
                                        (1) Pollard! no, b'ye blind?
(2) There, I do zee em over-right thik cow.
(3) The red woone?
                        (1) No, a mile beyand her now.
(3) Oh! there's the heäre, a-meäken vor the drong.
(2) My goodness! How the dogs do zweep along,
    A-poken out their pweinted noses' tips.
(3) He can't allow hizzelf much time vor slips!
(1) They'll hab 'en, after all, I'll bet a crown.
(2) Done vor a crown. They woon't! He's gwaïn to groun'.
(3) He is!
                (1) He idden!
                                (3) Ah! 'tis well his tooes
    Ha' got noo corns, inside o' hobnaïl shoes.
(1) He's geäme a-runnen too. Why, he do mwore
    Than eärn his life.

(3) His life wer his avore.
There, now the dogs wull turn en.
(2) No! He's right.
(1) He idden!
(2) Ees he is!
(3) He's out o' zight.
(1) Aye, aye. His mettle wull be well a-tried
A-gwaïn down Verny Hill, o' tother zide.
They'll have en there.
(3) O no! a vew good hops
Wull teäke en on to Knapton Lower Copse.
(2) An' that's a meesh that he've a-took avore.
(3) Ees, that's his hwome.
(1) He'll never reach his door.
(2) He wull.
(1) He woon't.
(3) Now, hark, d'ye hear em now?
(2) O! here's a bwoy a-come athirt the brow
O' Knapton Hill. We'll ax en.
(1) Here, my bwoy!
Can'st tell us where's the heäre?

Bwoy

He's got awoy.
(2) Ees, got awoy, in coo'se, I never zeed
A heäre a-scoten on wi' half his speed.
(1) Why, there, the dogs be wold, an' half a-done.
They can't catch anything wi' lags to run.
(2) Vrom vu'st to last they had but little chance
O' catchen o'n.
(3) They had a perty dance.
(1) No, catch en, no! I little thought they would;
He know'd his road too well to Knapton Wood.
(3) No! no! I wish the squier would let me feäre
On rabbits till his hounds do catch thik heäre.

WOAK HILL

When sycamore leaves wer a-spreaden,
   Green-ruddy, in hedges,
Bezide the red doust o' the ridges,
   A-dried at Woak Hill;

I packed up my goods all a-sheenen
   Wi' long years o' handlen,
On dousty red wheels ov a waggon,
   To ride at Woak Hill.

The brown thatchen ruf o' the dwellen
   I then wer a-leäven,
Had shelter'd the sleek head o' Meäry,
   My bride at Woak Hill.

But now vor zome years, her light voot-vall
   'S a-lost vrom the vlooren.
To soon vor my jaÿ an' my childern,
   She died at Woak Hill.

But still I do think that, in soul,
   She do hover about us;
To ho vor her motherless childern,
   Her pride at Woak Hill.

Zoo – lest she should tell me hereafter
   I stole off 'ithout her,
An' left her, uncall'd at house-ridden,
   To bide at Woak Hill –

I call'd her so fondly, wi' lippens
   All soundless to others,

An' took her wi' aïr-reachen hand,
  To my zide at Woak Hill.

On the road I did look round, a-talken
  To light at my shoulder,
An' then led her in at the door-way,
  Miles wide vrom Woak Hill.

An' that's why vo'k thought, vor a season,
  My mind wer a-wandren
Wi' sorrow, when I wer so sorely
  A-tried at Woak Hill.

But no; that my Meäry mid never
  Behold herzelf slighted,
I wanted to think that I guided
  My guide vrom Woak Hill.

GRAMMER A-CRIPPLED

'The zunny copse ha' birds to zing,
  The leäze ha' cows to low,
The elem trees ha' rooks on wing,
  The meäds a brook to flow,
But I can walk noo mwore, to pass
  The drashel out abrode,
To wear a path in theäse year's grass
  Or tread the wheelworn road,'
Cried Grammer. 'Then adieu,
      O runnen brooks,
      An' vlee-en rooks,
I can't come out to you.
If 'tis God's will, why then 'tis well,
That I should bide 'ithin a wall.'

An' then the childern, wild wi' fun,
An' loud wi' jaÿvul sounds,
Sprung in an' cried, 'We had a run,
A-plaÿen heäre an' hounds;
But oh! the cowslips where we stopt
In Maÿcreech, on the knap!'
An' vrom their little han's each dropt
Zome cowslips in her lap.
Cried Grammer, 'Only zee!
I can't teäke strolls,
An' little souls
Would bring the vields to me,
Since 'tis God's will, an' mus' be well
That I should bide 'ithin a wall.'

'Oh! there be prison walls to hold
The han's o' lawless crimes,
An' there be walls a-rear'd vor wold
An' zick in tryen times;
But oh! though low mid slant my ruf,
Though hard my lot mid be,
Though dry mid come my daily lwoaf,
Mid mercy leäve me free!'
Cried Grammer, 'Or adieu
To jaÿ, O grounds,
An' birds' gaÿ sounds
If I mus' gi'e up you;
Although 'tis well, in God's good will,
That I should bide 'ithin a wall.'

'Oh! then,' we answer'd, 'never fret,
If we shall be a-blest,
We'll work vull hard drough het an' wet
To keep your heart at rest:

The woaken chair's vor you to vill,
   Vor you shall glow the coal,
An' when the win' do whissle sh'ill
   We'll screen it vrom your poll.'
Cried Grammer, 'God is true.
         I can't but feel
         He smote to heal
My wounded heart in you;
An' zoo 'tis well, if 'tis His will,
That I be here 'ithin a wall.'

COME

Wull ye come in eärly Spring,
Come at Easter, or in Maÿ?
Or when Whitsuntide mid bring
Longer light to show your waÿ?
Wull ye come, if you be true,
Vor to quicken love anew?
Wull ye call in Spring or Fall?
Come now soon by zun or moon?
      Wull ye come?

Come wi' vaïce to vaïce the while
All their words be sweet to hear;
Come that feäce to feäce mid smile,
While their smiles do seem so dear;
Come within the year to seek
Woone you have sought woonce a week?
Come while flow'rs be on the bow'rs,
And the bird o' zong's a-heärd?
      Wull ye come?

Ees come *to* ye, an' come *vor* ye, is my word,
         I wull come.

LINDENORE

At Lindenore upon the steep,
Bezide the trees a-reachen high,
The while their lower limbs do zweep
The river-stream a-flowen by;
By graegle bells in beds o' blue,
Below the tree-stems in the lew,
Calm aïr do vind the rwose-bound door,
Ov Ellen Dare o' Lindenore.

An' there noo foam do hiss avore
Swift bwoats, wi' water-plowen keels,
An' there noo broad high-road's a-wore
By vur-brought trav'lers' cracklen wheels;
Noo crowd's a-passen to an' fro,
Upon the bridge's high-sprung bow:
An' vew but I do seek the door
Ov Ellen Dare o' Lindenore.

Vor there the town, wi' zun-bright walls,
Do sheen vur off, by hills o' grey,
An' town-vo'k ha' but seldom calls
O' business there, vrom day to day;
But Ellen didden leäve her ruf
To be admir'd, an' that's enough –
Vor I've a-vound 'ithin her door,
Feäir Ellen Dare o' Lindenore.

TOKENS

Green mwold on zummer bars do show
That they've a-dripp'd in Winter wet;
The hoof-worn ring o' groun' below

The tree, do tell o' storms or het;
The trees in rank along a ledge
Do show where woonce did bloom a hedge;
An' where the vurrow-marks do stripe
The down, the wheat woonce rustled ripe.
Each mark ov things a-gone vrom view –
To eyezight's woone, to soulzight two.

The grass ageän the mwoldren door
'S a token sad o' vo'k a-gone,
An' where the house, bwoth wall an' vloor,
'S a-lost, the well mid linger on.
What tokens, then, could Meäry gi'e
That she'd a'lived, an' liv'd vor me,
But things a-done vor thought an' view?
Good things that nwone ageän can do,
An' every work her love ha' wrought,
To eyezight's woone, but two to thought.

I'M OUT O' DOOR

I'm out, when, in the Winter's blast,
The zun, a-runnen lowly round,
Do mark the sheädes the hedge do cast
At noon, in hoarvrost, on the ground.
I'm out when snow's a-lyen white
In keen-aïr'd vields that I do pass,
An' moonbeams, vrom above, do smite
On ice an' sleeper's window-glass.
I'm out o' door,
When win' do zweep,
By hangen steep,
Or hollow deep,
At Lindenore.

O welcome is the lewth a-vound
By rustlen copse, or ivied bank,
Or by the haÿ-rick, weather-brown'd
By barken-grass, a-springen rank;
Or where the waggon, vrom the team
A-freed, is well a-housed vrom wet,
An' on the dousty cart-house beam
Do hang the cobweb's white-lin'd net;
While storms do roar,
An' win' do zweep,
By hangen steep,
Or hollow deep,
At Lindenore.

An' when a good day's work's a-done
An' I do rest, the while a squall
Do rumble in the hollow tun,
An' ivy-stems do whip the wall,
Then in the house do sound about
My ears, dear vaïces vull or thin,
A-praÿen vor the souls vur out
At sea, an' cry wi' bibb'ren chin –
Oh ! shut the door.
What soul can sleep,
Upon the deep,
When storms do zweep
At Lindenore.

SHAFTESBURY FEAIR

When hillborne Paladore did show
So bright to me down miles below,
As woonce the zun, a-rollen west,
Did brighten up his hill's high breast,
Wi' walls a-looken dazzlen white,
Or yellow, on the grey-topp'd height

Ov Paladore, as peäle day wore
Away so feäir;
Oh ! how I wish'd that I wer there.

The pleäce wer too vur off to spy
The liven vo'k a-passen by;
The vo'k too vur vor aïr to bring
The words that they did speak or zing.
All dum' to me wer each abode,
An' empty wer the down-hill road
Vrom Paladore, as peäle day wore
Away so feäir,
But how I wish'd that I wer there.

But when I clomb the lofty ground
Where liven veet an' tongues did sound,
At feäir, bezide your bloomen feäce,
The pertiest in all the pleäce,
As you did look, wi' eyes as blue
As yonder southern hills in view,
Vrom Paladore – O Polly dear,
Wi' you up there,
How merry then wer I at feäir.

Since vu'st I trod thik steep hill-zide
My grieven soul 'v a-been a-tried
Wi' païn, an' loss o' worldly gear,
An' souls a-gone I wanted near;
But you be here to goo up still,
An' look to Blackmwore vrom the hill
O' Paladore. Zoo, Polly dear,
We'll goo up there,
An' spend an hour or two at feäir.

The wold brown meäre's a-brought vrom grass,
An' rubb'd an' cwomb'd so bright as glass;
An' now we'll hitch her in, an' start

To feäir upon the new green cart,
An' teäke our little Poll between
Our zides, as proud's a little queen,
To Paladore. Aye, Poll a dear,
        Vor now 'tis feäir,
An' she's a-longen to goo there.

While Paladore, on watch, do straïn
Her eyes to Blackmwore's blue-hill'd pläin,
While Duncliffe is the traveller's mark,
Or cloty Stour's a-rollen dark;
Or while our bells do call, vor greäce,
The vo'k avore their Seävior's feäce,
Mid Paladore, an' Poll a dear,
        Vor ever know
O' peace and plenty down below.

A LOT OF MAIDENS A-RUNNEN THE VIELDS

'Come on. Be sprack, a-laggen back.'
'Oh! be there any cows to hook?'
'Lauk she's afraïd, a silly maïd.
Cows? No, the cows be down by brook.'
'O here then, oh! here is a lot.'
'A lot o' what? what is it? what?'
'Why blackberries, as thick
As ever they can stick.'
'I've dewberries, oh! twice
As good as they; so nice.'
'Look here. Theäse boughs be all but blue
Wi' snags.'
        'Oh! gi'e me down a vew.'
'Come here, oh! do but look.'
'What's that? what is it now?'
'Why nuts a-slippen shell.'
'Hee! hee! pull down the bough.'

'I wish I had a crook.'
'There zome o'm be a-vell.'
(*One sings*)
'I wish I was on Bimport Hill;
I would zit down and cry my vill.'

'Hee! hee! there's Jenny zomewhere nigh,
A-zingen that she'd like to cry.'

(*Jenny sings*)
'I would zit down and cry my vill
Until my tears would dreve a mill.'

'Oh! here's an ugly crawlen thing,
A sneäke.'
'A slooworm; he won't sting.'
'Hee! hee! how she did squal an' hop,
A-spinnen roun' so quick's a top.'
'Look here, oh! quick, be quick.'
'What is it? what then? where?'
'A rabbit.'
'No, a heäre.'
'Ooh! ooh! the thorns do prick.'
'How he did scote along the ground
As if he wer avore a hound.'
'Now mind the thistles.'
'Hee, hee, hee,
Why there be knapweeds.'
'No.'
'They be.'
'I've zome'hat in my shoe.'
'Zit down, an' sheäke it out.'
'Oh! emmets, oh! ooh, ooh,
A-crawlen all about.'
'What bird is that, O harken, hush.
How sweetly he do zing.'
'A nightengeäle.'

'La ! no, a drush.'
'Oh ! here's a funny thing.'
'Oh ! how the bull do hook,
An' bleäre, an' fling the dirt.'
'Oh ! won't he come athirt?'
'No, he's beyond the brook.'
'O lauk ! a hornet rose
Up clwose avore my nose.'
'Oh ! what wer that so white
Rush'd out o' thik tree's top?'
'An owl.'
'How I did hop,
How I do sheäke wi' fright.'
'A musheroom.'
'O lau !
A twoadstool ! Pwoison ! Augh.'
'What's that, a mouse?'
'O no,
Teäke ceäre, why 'tis a shrow.'
'Be sure don't let en come
An' run athirt your shoe;
He'll meäke your voot so numb
That you won't veel a tooe.'
'Oh ! what wer that so loud
A-rumblen?'
'Why a clap
O' thunder. Here's a cloud
O' raïn. I veel a drap.'
'A thunderstorm. Do raïn.
Run hwome wi' might an' maïn.'
'Hee ! hee ! oh ! there's a drop
A-trickled down my back. Hee ! hee !'
'My head's as wet's a mop.'
'Oh ! thunder !'
'There's a crack. Oh ! Oh !'

'Oh! I've a-got the stitch, Oh!'
'Oh! I've a-lost my shoe, Oh!'
'There's Fanny into ditch, Oh!'
'I'm wet all drough an' drough, Oh!'

WHICH ROAD?

Still green on the limbs o' the woak wer the leaves,
Where the black slooe did grow, a-meal'd over wi' grey,
Though leäzes, a-burnt, wer wi' bennets a-brown'd,
An' the stubble o' wheat wer a-witheren white,
While sooner the zunlight did zink vrom the zight,
An' longer did linger the dim-roaded night.

But bright wer the day-light a-dryen the dew,
As foam wer a-villen the pool in its vall,
An' a-sheenen did climb, by the chalk o' the cliff,
The white road a-voun' steep to the waweary step,
Where along by the knap, wi' a high-beätèn breast,
Went the maïd an' the chap to the feäst in their best.

There hosses went by wi' their neck in a bow,
An' did toss up their nose over outspringen knees;
An' the ox, heäiryhided, wi' low-swingen head;
An' the sheep, little knee'd, wi' a quick-dippen nod;
An' a maïd, wi' her head a-borne on in a proud
Gaït o' walken, so smooth as an aïr-zwimmen cloud.

WALKEN HWOME AT NIGHT

You then vor me meäde up your mind
To leäve your rights o' hwome behind,
Your width o' teäble-rim an' bit
O' virezide vloor, where you did zit,
An' all your walks by stiles an' geätes
O' summer vields wi' maïden meätes,
To guide vor me my house, though small,

A-reckon'd, all my house mid be.
Come, hood your head; the wind is keen.
Come this zide, here. I'll be your screen.

The clothes your mother put ye on
Be now a-worn all out an' gone,
An' you do wear vrom top to tooe
What my true love ha' bought ye new,
That now in comely sheäpe's a-shown,
My own a-decken ov my own;
An' oh! ov all that I've a-got,
Vor your sweet lot a half is small.
Come, hood your head; wrap up, now do.
Walk clwose to me. I'll keep ye lew.

An' now when we be out to spend
A vrosty night wi' zome wold friend,
An' ringen clocks to tell at last
The evenen hour's a-gone too vast,
Noo vorked roads, to left an' right,
Do sunder us vor night or light;
But all my woe's vor you to veel,
An' all my weal's vor you to know.
Come, hood your head. You can't zee out?
I'll leäd ye right, you needen doubt.

THE WOLD CLOCK

The wold clock's feäce is still in pleäce,
Wi' hands a-stealen round,
His bob do swing an' bell do ring,
As when I heärd his sound,

A-leäven hwome, so long a-gone,
An' left en there, a-ticken on.

Noo doust do clog, noo rust uncog
His wheels to keep em still,
Noo blow ha' vell to crack his bell
That still do ringle shrill.
I wish that I'd a-gone so well
'S the clock's wold bob, an' wheels, an' bell.

Who now do wind his chaïn, a-twin'd
As he do run his hours,
Or meäke a gloss to sheen across
His door, wi' goolden flow'rs,
Since he've a-sounded out the last
Still hours our dear good mother pass'd?

THE WIND UP THE STREAM

The sheäded stream did run below
Tall elems, on the bank, in row,
That leafy ivy stems did clim'
In light a-shot vrom limb to limb:
An' winds did plaÿ, now brisk, now slack,
All up the stream, a-drevèn back
The runnen weäves; an' meäke em seem
To be an upward-flowen stream:
As hope do zometimes meäke us think
Our life do rise, the while do zink.

LOWSHOT LIGHT

As I went eastward, while the zun did zet,
His yollow light on bough by bough did sheen.

An' there, among the gil'cups by the knap,
Below the elems, cow by cow did sheen.

While after heäiry-headed horses' heels,
Wi' slowly-rollen wheels, the plough did sheen.

An' up among the vo'k upon the reäves,
One lovely feäce, wi' zunny brow, did sheen.

An' bright, vor that one feäce, the bough, an' cow,
An' plough, in my sweet fancy, now do sheen.

GREEN

Our zummer way to church did wind about
The cliff, where ivy on the ledge wer green.

Our zummer way to town did skirt the wood,
Where sheenen leaves in tree an' hedge wer green.

Our zummer way to milken in the meäd,
Wer on by brook, where fluttren zedge wer green.

Our hwomeward ways did all run into one,
Where moss upon the roofstwones' edge wer green.

SHELLBROOK

Then out at Shellbrook, roun' by stile an' tree,
Wi' longer days an' zunny hours a-come,
Wi' spring an' all the zunny show'rs a-come,
Wi' Maÿ an' all its sheenen flow'rs a-come,
How sweet vor young wi' young to meet in glee.

An' there how we in merry talk did goo
By foam below the river baÿ, all white,
By blossom on the green-leaved Maÿ, all white,
By chalk bezide the dousty waÿ, all white,
Where glitt'ren waters match'd the sky wi' blue.

Or else in winden paths by vield or drong,
We over knaps a-slopen steep did wind,
Or down the dells a-zinken deep did wind,
Or where the benden brook did zweep did wind,
All young wi' young in merry laugh or zong.

But now the winter-vrozen churchyard wall do keep
The plot o' tower-sheäded ground all white,
Where friends can vind the vrosted mound, all white,
Wi' turf a-zwellen up so round, all white
Wi' young a-sunder'd vrom the young in sleep.

A BRISK WIND

The burdock leaves upon the ledge,
The leaves upon the poplar's height,
A-blown by wind all up on edge,
Did show their underzides o' white;
An' withy trees bezide the rocks

Did bend grey limbs, did swaÿ grey boughs,
As there, on waggen heads, dark locks
Bespread red cheäks, behung white brows.

WINTER A-COMEN

I'm glad we have wood in store awhile,
Avore all the ground's avrore awhile;
Vor soon we must shut the door awhile
Vrom wind that's a-whirlen snow.

The zwallows have all a-hied away,
The flowers have now a-died away,
An' boughs, wi' their leaves a-dried away,
In wind do goo to an' fro.

Your walks in the ash-tree droves be cwold,
Your banks in the elem groves be cwold,
Your bench by the house's oves be cwold
Where zummer did leätely glow.

Noo rwose is a-bloomen red to-day,
Noo pink vor your breast or head to-day,
A-decken the geärden bed to-day,
Do linger a-nodden low.

Noo mwore is the swingen lark above,
An' aïr all a-clouded dark above
Do stifle the zun's last spark above,
Where little blue sky do show.

Zoo now gi'e your cheäks a bloom to-night,
Where vier do het the room to-night,

A-drevèn away the gloom to-night,
While winterly wind do blow.

WHITE AN' BLUE

My love is o' comely height, an' straïght,
An' comely in all her ways an' gaït;
In feäce she do show the rwose's hue,
An' her lids on her eyes be white on blue.

When Elemley clubmen walk'd in Maÿ
An' vo'k come in clusters, ev'ry waÿ,
As soon as the zun dried up the dew,
An' clouds in the sky wer white on blue,

She come by the down, wi' trippen walk,
By deäisies, an' sheenen banks o' chalk,
An' brooks, where the crowvoot flow'rs did strew
The sky-tinted water, white on blue.

She nodded her head, as plaÿ'd the band;
She dapp'd wi' her voot, as she did stand;
She danced in a reel, a-wearen new
A skirt wi' a jacket, white wi' blue.

I singled her out vrom thin an' stout,
Vrom slender an' stout I chose her out;
An' what, in the evenen, could I do,
But gi'e her my breast-knot, white an' blue?

FOR A MARRIAGE

The oneness of wedlock, by Christ,
Has from earthly been blest to divine,
As the water that once, by His word,
Was, at Cana, all turn'd into wine.

And the wedding of two holy lives
Into one, in the name of the Son,
Still betokens the blending in Him
Of the Godhead and manhood in one.

Let the wife ever honor the man,
And the man ever love his own wife;
As the Savior so lovèd his church
That He *for* her upgave His own life.

Let the husband and wife, as one flesh,
Have one life, and one home, and one name,
And one honor, one weal, and one woe,
One God, and one hope, and one aim.

Never let them be ever more twain
Until one shall have drawn the last breath;
And be lovely and blest in their lives,
To be blest in a life beyond death.

THE EEGRASS

With stricken heart, and melting mood,
I rov'd along the mead to brood
In freedom, at the eventide,
On souls that time has scatter'd wide;

As by the boughy hedge's side
    The shadows darken'd into night,
    And cooling airs, with wanton flight,
        Were blowing o'er the eegrass.

There fancy roam'd from place to place,
From year to year, to find some face
That I no more shall look upon,
Or see in sadness, sorrow-wan,
Or time-worn with its brightness gone;
    And my own Lucy, fair to see,
    Seem'd there to come again to me,
        Up o'er the shining eegrass.

As when upon a summer's day,
While we were there at hawling hay,
With downcast look she lightly drew
Her rake-head to her shapely shoe,
With hands well skill'd to bring it through
    The tangled crowfoot-stems, that broke
    The rakes for us poor clumsy folk,
        And still are in the eegrass.

And there the storms that spring clouds shed
Fell lately on her hooded head,
The while she sat, at eventide,
A-milking by her dun cow's side;
And there, when summer, sunny-skied
    And boughy-wooded, brought its heat,
    She trod the flow'rs with light-shod feet,
        But comes not o'er the eegrass.

O summer all thy crops are down,
And copse and leaze are turning brown,

And cuckoos leave the boughs to fade
Through waning fall, within the glade;
And we have lost our blooming maid.
  So all thou broughtest fresh and fair
  Begins to wither ev'ry where,
    But this bright-bladed eegrass.

A WINTER NIGHT

It was a chilly winter's night;
  And frost was glitt'ring on the ground,
And evening stars were twinkling bright;
  And from the gloomy plain around
      Came no sound,
But where, within the wood-girt tow'r,
The churchbell slowly struck the hour;

As if that all of human birth
  Had risen to the final day,
And soaring from the wornout earth
  Were called in hurry and dismay,
      Far away;
And I alone of all mankind
Were left in loneliness behind.

THE MAID THAT I HAVE WON

The winning maid that I have won
Of womankind's the very sun,
That in her dazzling day-light hides
The duller maids I know besides,

Like twinkling stars all wan and weak
That wane from morning's golden streak.
Her soul's as pure's the lofty light
The lark sings in at greatest height;
Her love's as true as low-cast shades
To lofty suns above the glades;
And she is to be woo'd and won
By one alone below the sun;
And God has met my heart to make
A maid so fair for my poor sake,
And did not either bring her on
For eyes of generations gone,
Or leave her longer back, to shine
In later days than these of mine,
But raised her ripening now to be
So rich a prize alone for me.

MY DEAREST JULIA

Oh! can or can I not live on,
Forgetting thee, my love forgone?
'Tis true, where joyful faces crowd
And merry tongues are ringing loud,
Or where some needful work unwrought
May call for all my care and thought,
Or where some landscape, bath'd in light,
May spread to fascinate my sight,
Thy form may melt awhile, as fade
Our shades within some welkin shade,
    And I awhile may then live on,
    Forgetting thee, my love forgone.

But then the thrilling thought comes on,
    Of all thy love that's now forgone;
Thy daily toil to earn me wealth,
Thy grief to see me out of health,
Thy yearning readiness to share
The burden of my toil and care,
And all the blessings thou hast wrought
In my behalf by deed and thought.
And then I seem to hear thee calling,
Gloomy fac'd with tear drops falling,
    'Canst thou then so soon live on,
    Forgetful of my love forgone?'

COME AND MEET ME

Husband to Wife

Well, to-day then I shall roll off on the road
Round by Woodcombs, out to Shellbrook, to the mill;
With my brand-new little spring-cart, with a load,
To come loadless round by Chalk-hill, at my will:
As the whole day will be dry,
By the tokens of the sky,
Come to meet me, with the children, on the road.

For the sunshine from the blue sky's hollow height,
Now is glitt'ring on the stream-wave and the sedge;
And the orchard is a broad sheet of the white
Of new blossom over blossom on the hedge:
So when clock-bells ring out four,
Let them send you out of door,
Come to meet me, with the children, on the road.

You can saunter, if I'm lated by the clock,
To some blue-bells for the children on the ridge;
Or can loiter by the tree-shades, on the rock
Where the water tumbles headlong by the bridge:
While the boy's line and his hook
May catch minnows in the brook,
Out to meet me, with his sister, on the road.

You may dawdle for a furlong on a-head,
And be welcome at the Weldons, on the knap,
Where the cowslips are so close grown in a bed,
That our Poll's hands will have soon fill'd up her lap,
For a toss-ball up as big
As her small head's curly wig,
Out to meet me, with her brother, on the road.

At the time, then, I have told you, you may hear
My two wheel-rims and four horse-shoes on the road,
And the spring-cart with the seat up, near and near,
To spin you home, with the children, for its load.
So come out, then, to the sun
With the children for a run:
Come and meet me, with the children, on the road.

BENIGHTED

Invited by your sire's good will
  To me, I took the road
By Downley, over heath and hill,
  To go to your abode;
And o'er my mare, as white as snow,
  Full fain I sprightly threw
My leg, and in my stirrup's bow

I set my shining shoe,
And merry-hearted,
Briskly started
Out by our old yew.

But when, at last, the sun had set
Upon my road, too soon,
I found myself where three ways met
Below the western moon.
There stood a shining holly tree,
With firs of five-fold height,
But yet no guide-post held for me
An arm to send me right,
As I benighted,
Moon-belighted,
Turn'd my wheeling sight.

And one road down a ground-slope sank,
A darken'd, hollow way;
And one beside a heathy bank
Ran on as light as day;
And nigh it wound a shining brook,
Adown a shallow bed,
And thitherward my mare would look
With ever-steadfast head,
As if well knowing,
Without showing,
Whitherward I sped.

And shortly, from the eastern sky,
I found five bell-sounds sweep;
Your peal of bells – one shrill, one high,
One loud, one low, one deep –
And with my moonshade on before

My mare's two ears' white tips,
I soon had reached your gate, your door,
Your fire of blazing chips,
Where I, at meeting,
Found a greeting,
Out of many lips.

I never after that mistook
The right road of the three,
And well I knew the shallow brook,
And firs, and holly tree;
I ne'er mistook the road when day
Show'd houses from afar,
Nor when the moon was o'er my way,
Nor by the evening star,
As I rode spanking
On by banking,
Gapp'd for gate or bar.

THE PASSING NIGHT

The cloud-hidden sun had lately set
On hill as on dell outreaching dark,
And mist, on the sweeping wind, came wet
O'er quivering leaves and ribby bark;
The while, by the fire outglowing red
And flame of the lamp upspearing white,
Good folk, with a roof above their head,
Now let the night go; let go the night.

And where the still bird was in the dry,
Or where the shy ground-beast shunn'd the drops,
Or which under cliff or roof might lie,
Or which in the rick, or grove, or copse

I knew not, nor cared I where the dove
  Was gone to her roost, all out of sight;
But still I may find (thought I) my love
  The while the night goes; while goes the night.

And strong was the wind throughout the mile,
  And misty it blew on slope and ridge,
And swiftly it sped through gate and stile,
  And swept o'er the stream below the bridge.
But still if I reach (thought I) the door
  Before they put out the fire and light,
And ere they may leave the old hall-floor,
  Then let the night blow; let blow the night.

The children's light feet had climb'd the treads
  Of stairs that to them are high and steep,
And lay on their darksome little beds
  With white little eyelids shut in sleep.
But there is the eldest child of all,
  And now has upgrown to woman's height,
And sits with her elders in the hall
  The while the night goes; while goes the night.

TROUBLES OF THE DAY

As there, along the elmy hedge, I go
  By banksides white with parsley – parsley-bloom –
Where smell of new-mown hay comes wafted by
  On wind of dewy evening, evening gloom,
And homeward take my shaded way between
The hedge's high-tipp'd wood, and barley green,
      I sing, or mean
'O troubles of the day. Flee to the west,
Come not my homeward way. I seek my rest.'

The dairy cows, by meadow trees, lie free
   Of calls to milkers' pails – the milkmaids' calls;
The horses now have left their rolling wheels
   And reel'd in home to stable, to their stalls,
And down the grey-pool'd stream the fish awhile
Are free from all the prowling angler's guile,
         And o'er the stile
I sink, and sing or say, 'Flee to the west
O troubles of the day. I seek my rest.'

My boy – whose little high-rigged boat, athwart
   The windy pool, by day, at afternoon,
Has fluttered, tippling like a bird
   That tries to fly unfledged, to fly too soon –
Now sleeps forgetful of the boat, and fond
Old dog that he had taught to swim the pond.
         So flee beyond
The edge of sinking day, towards the west,
Ye troubles flee away. I seek my rest.

A star is o'er the tower on the hill,
   Whence rings no clanging knell, no evening peal;
The mill stands dark beside the flouncing foam;
   But still is all its gear, its mossy wheel.
No rooks now sweep along the darkened sky,
And o'er the road few feet or wheels go by.
         So fly, O fly
Ye troubles, with the day, adown the west,
Come not along my way. I seek my rest.

FORETHINGS FOR AFTER ONES

The stone of our new wall
   Within the rock unbroken lay

Ere man had lifted to the day
A stone to build at all;
But though, to men unknown,
It lay asleep in darksome beds,
'Twas yet to shelter our two heads
That lay that hidden stone.

The gold that's in your ring
Lay mingled in the rock with sand,
Unreach'd by man's tool-wielding hand,
Ere we were anything;
Ere liv'd a smith to mould
A jewel by the helping flame,
For you ere gold had yet a name
Was kept that hidden gold.

The Mind of minds, with sight
That seeth all things as in one,
And all things yet undone as done,
Thus guideth all things right.
To nothing ever blind,
He fitteth wisely from afar
For things that are not, those that are,
An all beholding mind.

BLACK AND WHITE

By the wall of the garden, that glimmer'd chalk white
In the light of the moon, back in May,
There were you all in black at my side, coming round
On the ground with a cypress to sway:
Oh! the white and the black! Which was fairest to view?
Why the black became fairest on you.

By the water, downfalling in many a bow
White as snow, on the rock's peaky steep,
There your own petted cow show'd the ridge of her back
Of deep black, as she lay for her sleep :
Oh ! the white and the black ! Which was fairest to view ?
Why the black became fairest on you.

When you stroll'd down the village at evening, bedight
All in white, in the warm summer-tide,
The while *Towsy,* your loving old dog, with his back
Sleeky black, trotted on at your side :
Ah ! the black and the white ! Which was fairest to view ?
Why the white became fairest on you.

At the end of the barton the granary stood,
Of black wood, with white geese at its side,
And the white-winged swans glided over the waves
By the cave's darksome shadows in pride :
Oh ! the black and the white ! Which was fairest to view ?
Why the white became fairest on you.

THE GEATE A-VALLEN TO

In the zunsheen ov our summers
  Wi' the haÿ time now a-come,
How busy wer we out a-vield
  Wi' vew a-left at hwome,
When waggons rumbled out ov yard
  Red wheeled, wi' body blue,
As back behind 'em loudly slamm'd
  The geäte a-vallèn to.

Drough daysheen ov how many years
  The geäte ha' now a-swung
Behind the veet o' vull-grown men
  An' vootsteps ov the young.
Drough years o' days it swung to us
  Behind each little shoe,
As we tripped lightly on avore
  The geäte a-vallèn to.

In evenen time o' starry night
  How mother zot at hwome,
An' kept her bleäzen vire bright
  Till father should ha' come,
An' how she quicken'd up an' smiled
  An' stirred her vire anew,
To hear the trampen ho'ses' steps
  An' geäte a-vallèn to.

There's moon-sheen now in nights o' fall
  When leaves be brown vrom green,
When, to the slammen o' the geäte,
  Our Jenny's ears be keen,
When the wold dog do wag his taïl,
  An' Jeän could tell to who,
As he do come in drough the geäte,
  The geäte a-vallèn to.

An' oft do come a saddened hour
  When there must goo away
One well-beloved to our heart's core,
  Vor long, perhaps vor aye :
An' oh ! it is a touchen thing
  The loven heart must rue,
To hear within his last farewell
  The geäte a-vallèn to.

GLOSSARY

A-coath'd, diseased in the liver
Athirt, athwart
Avore, before
Ax, ask
Barken, barton, stock yard or cow yard
Bavens, faggots of long brushwood
Bennets, flower-stalks of grass
Bissen, thou bist not
Blooth, blossom
Car, to carry
Clote, yellow water-lily
Dather, to bewilder
Doust, dust
Drashel, threshold
Dree, three
Drong, narrow way
Drough, through
Drush, thrush
Eegrass, aftermath
Eltrot, cowparsley
Emmet, ant
Gil'cups, buttercups
Girt, great
Goo, go
Graegle, bluebell
Het, heat
He'th, hearth
Hile, pile of sheaves
Ho, to feel a weight of care
Kern, to grow into fruit
Kexes, stems of hemlock or cowparsley
Kitty-boots, low laced boots

Knap, hillock
Leäne, lane
Leäse, leäze, unmown field, stocked through spring and summer
Lew, sheltered from the wind
Lewth, lewness
Litsome, gay
Nitch, load
Oves, eaves
Pank, to pant
Parrock, paddock
Pooke, a cone of weales of hay
Reaves, ladder-like framework on the sides of a waggon
Roller, ridge of hay
Ruf, roof
Ruffen, roofing
Shrow, shrew mouse
Skimmy, to cut off tufts of grass
Sprack, quick
Stunpoles, blockheads
Sumple, supple
Taït, to play see-saw
Ted, to throw the hay abroad to dry
Theäsem, these
Tod, load
Tutty, nosegay
Vlee, fly
Vo'k, folk
Vuzz, furze
Weäle, big ridge of dried hay
Whiver, to hover, quiver
Zwath, swath

INDEX OF FIRST LINES